GRAHAM LINEHAM

CRAFTING COMEDY, SHAPING CULTURE

WRITTEN BY:
MAURIE PUTELLA

TABLE OF CONTENTS

PREFACE

Graham Linehan, a prominent figure in the world of Irish comedy writing, is a man of multifaceted talents and convictions. Born in 1968, his creative contributions have left an indelible mark on the landscape of television comedy. Yet, beyond his comedy accolades, Linehan has become a polarizing figure due to his involvement in anti-transgender activism, sparking a contentious dialogue on the subject.

Among his notable achievements, Linehan holds the distinction of creating or co-creating several beloved sitcoms, including the iconic "Father Ted" (1995–1998), the hilariously offbeat "Black Books" (2000–2004), and the tech-savvy gem "The IT Crowd" (2006–2013). His wit and storytelling prowess have also graced other shows such as "Count Arthur Strong," "Brass Eye," and "The Fast Show." This formidable body of work earned him recognition in the form of five prestigious BAFTA awards, including the coveted Best Writer, Comedy, for "The IT Crowd" in 2014.

However, Linehan's career trajectory took an unexpected turn when an episode of "The IT Crowd" faced criticism for its perceived transphobia. This marked the genesis of his involvement in the contentious realm of anti-transgender activism. Linehan firmly asserts that transgender activism poses a threat to women's safety, a viewpoint that has ignited heated debates. He has taken his stance further by drawing a provocative parallel, likening the use of puberty blockers to the dark specter of Nazi eugenics. This analogy has stirred controversy and intensified the discourse surrounding gender identity and healthcare choices.

In the midst of this ideological maelstrom, Linehan has positioned himself as a self-professed victim of cancel culture. He contends that his outspoken views have exacted a toll on his professional life, claiming to have lost work opportunities and, perhaps even more significantly, experiencing the dissolution of his marriage as a result of his advocacy. In this complex narrative, Graham Linehan's trajectory spans from a celebrated comedy writer to a controversial figure in the fraught arena of transgender rights, where his creative genius and activist fervor continue to intersect and collide.

EARLY LIFE AND EDUCATION

Graham Linehan's journey begins in the heart of Dublin, where he came into the world in 1968. His formative years were shaped by his education and early experiences in the vibrant Irish capital.

His educational odyssey commenced at Plunkett's School, situated in the Whitehall district of Dublin's north side. Here, amidst the city's bustling streets and rich cultural tapestry, Linehan began to lay the foundation for his future endeavors.

Subsequently, he ventured into the realm of secondary education at Catholic University School, a prestigious Roman Catholic institution for young boys located in Dublin. This chapter of his life not only nurtured his intellect but also provided a cultural and religious backdrop that would later influence his work.

Before embarking on his illustrious career in comedy and writing, Linehan made a pivotal stop at Hot Press, a renowned Irish music and entertainment magazine. This engagement with the world of media likely played a role in shaping his creative sensibilities and passion for storytelling, setting the stage for the remarkable contributions he would make to the world of television comedy in the years to come.

PERSONAL LIFE

The narrative of Graham Linehan's personal life is a tapestry woven with both love and advocacy, featuring a union that transcends familial ties and a deeply impactful campaign.

In the year 2004, Linehan took a significant step in his personal journey by marrying Helen Serafinowicz, a writer whose connection to the world of entertainment was further solidified by her familial bond to the actor Peter Serafinowicz. Their union represented the merging of creative spirits, bound by the shared path they were destined to embark upon.

This partnership bore fruit in the form of two beloved children, bestowing upon them the joys and responsibilities of parenthood. Their family life unfolded against the backdrop of Norwich, a picturesque city in England that would serve as their home, nurturing their bonds and shaping their experiences.

Yet, beyond the realm of personal joys, Linehan and Helen found themselves standing on the precipice of a profound and impactful moment in their lives. In October 2015, they lent their voices and convictions to a collaboration with Amnesty International, a human rights organization dedicated to championing causes close to their hearts.

Their shared endeavor centered on a campaign film, a powerful call to action urging the Irish government to repeal the Eighth Amendment of the Constitution. This amendment recognized the right to life of the unborn while acknowledging the equal right to life of the mother, thus influencing the nation's laws.

What made this campaign deeply personal was Linehan and Helen's revelation. They bravely shared their decision to terminate a pregnancy due to acrania while residing in England back in 2004. Their story cast a harsh light on the fact that, had they been in Ireland at the time, undergoing such a procedure would have been deemed an offense, carrying a staggering maximum prison sentence of 14 years. Their advocacy became a poignant testimony to the critical need for reform in the realm of reproductive rights, and it underscored the profound impact that their own lived experience had on their unwavering commitment to the cause.

In the midst of their love story and their creative endeavors, Linehan and Helen's collaboration with Amnesty International stands as a testament to their determination to effect change and to lend their voices to the causes that resonate deeply within their hearts.

The evolution of Graham Linehan's personal journey carries with it both triumphs and tribulations, echoing the ebb and flow of life's complexities.

In the annals of his personal history, 2020 marked a pivotal juncture. It was the year when Linehan's marriage to Helen Serafinowicz reached its conclusion, the bonds strained by the weight of his anti-transgender activism. This shift in his personal life led him to make a geographical move, finding himself in the bustling metropolis of London, a city of endless possibilities and change.

The fractures in their relationship weren't solely attributed to ideological differences. Linehan candidly revealed that his legal and financial challenges, coupled with unnerving visits from law enforcement, cast a shadow over their partnership. The pressures and demands of his activism had taken a toll on their union, further highlighting the personal sacrifices he had made in pursuit of his beliefs.

Compounding his personal trials, Linehan disclosed a struggle with anxiety that had persisted for half a decade or more. The catalyst for this inner turmoil stemmed from the legal threats he had received from trans rights activists. The toll this took on his mental well-being underscores the personal cost he bore for his staunch convictions.

In matters of faith, Linehan identifies as an atheist, a perspective he has championed publicly. His involvement in the Atheist Bus Campaign in January 2009 was an influential moment in his advocacy for secularism. His voice joined the chorus of those advocating for a more secular society, and he became an honorary associate of the National Secular Society, further cementing his commitment to the cause.

As life unfolded, Linehan's personal resilience was put to the test once more in 2018 when he faced a formidable adversary—testicular cancer. Despite the daunting diagnosis, he emerged victorious from successful surgery, a testament to his unwavering determination to overcome life's challenges.

In the narrative of Graham Linehan's life, the interplay of personal convictions, emotional trials, and medical triumphs paints a portrait of a multifaceted individual whose journey continues to unfold, marked by both resilience and a steadfast commitment to the causes that resonate with him.

Graham Linehan's digital presence, notably on Twitter, forms an integral part of his persona and engagement with the world. In a revealing 2015 interview, he described Twitter as nothing short of "part of [his] nervous system," underlining its significance in his daily life.

One of his earliest forays into Twitter's interactive landscape took place on 13 February 2009 when Linehan initiated the inaugural "BadMovieClub" event. This unique Twitter gathering, which he hosted, invited users to partake in lively discussions about poorly-rated films. The concept gained such traction that it was reprised the following day at midnight, with comedian Phill Jupitus taking on the hosting duties.

In August 2009, Linehan once again harnessed the power of Twitter, this time in response to criticism of the United Kingdom's National Health Service (NHS) by members of the United States Republican Party. His response was the creation of the hashtag-driven campaign #welovetheNHS. This digital rallying cry quickly became a platform for individuals to express their unwavering support for the NHS, demonstrating the potential of social media as a vehicle for advocacy.

However, Linehan's Twitter engagement was not solely confined to the realm of social and political issues. In 2011, he perpetrated a Twitter hoax that reverberated across the digital landscape. Linehan humorously suggested that the notorious Osama bin Laden was a fan of "The IT Crowd," a clever jest that showcased his irreverent and comedic side while garnering attention and laughter from his online audience.

Throughout his digital journey, Graham Linehan's Twitter presence has served as both a platform for his creative ideas and a medium for his social and political activism. It highlights his ability to navigate the digital age while staying true to his unique brand of humor and social consciousness.

COMEDY CAREER

Collaboration With Authur Mathews

The creative partnership between Graham Linehan and Arthur Mathews traces its origins back to their early days at Hot Press, a platform where their shared creative energies first ignited. This fortuitous encounter would lead to a prolific collaboration that would span across the landscape of British television comedy.

Their initial joint endeavors found them crafting memorable segments for various sketch shows, including comedy stalwarts like "Alas Smith and Jones," "Harry Enfield & Chums," "The All New Alexei Sayle Show," "The Day Today," and the iconic Ted and Ralph characters in "The Fast Show." Their comedic synergy and knack for crafting humor that resonated with audiences quickly became evident.

Their creative partnership matured and evolved as they continued to join forces on various projects. One such endeavor was "Paris," a series that bore their distinct comedic fingerprint, albeit for a single series in 1994. However, their most enduring legacy would be the beloved sitcom "Father Ted," which graced screens for three series from 1995 to 1998. This iconic show, set on the fictional Craggy Island, became a staple of British and Irish comedy, showcasing their unparalleled talent for crafting humor that transcended boundaries.

The duo's collaborative genius also found expression in the first series of the sketch show "Big Train," adding to their impressive body of work. Furthermore, they penned the memorable "Dearth of a Salesman" episode for the series "Coogan's Run," featuring the comically inept character Gareth Cheeseman, who left audiences in stitches with his bumbling antics.

Their comedic prowess did not go unnoticed, as in late 2003, Linehan and Mathews earned a well-deserved accolade. They were recognized as one of the 50 funniest acts to grace the television landscape by "The Observer," a testament to their enduring impact on the world of comedy.

The pinnacle of their collaborative efforts was "Father Ted," which garnered not just laughter but critical acclaim. This timeless sitcom clinched BAFTA awards for Best Comedy in both 1996 and 1999, solidifying its place in the pantheon of British television classics. The enduring charm and wit of "Father Ted" stand as a testament to the indomitable creative spirit of Linehan and Mathews, two comedic maestros who forever left their mark on the world of humor.

LATER COLLABORATIONS AND LEGACIES

Graham Linehan's creative footprint in the world of comedy extends across an impressive array of projects, each a testament to his distinctive voice and sharp wit.

In 1997, Linehan made his mark as a writer on the satirical series "Brass Eye," a show known for its incisive take on contemporary issues. He also contributed to "Blue Jam" from 1997 to 1999, a program defined by its subversive and offbeat humor, and "Jam" in 2000, another foray into the realm of unconventional comedy.

One of Linehan's most celebrated collaborations came to fruition alongside actor Dylan Moran when they co-created the beloved sitcom "Black Books." This partnership birthed a show that ran from 2000 to 2004, characterized by its quirky humor and unforgettable characters.

However, Linehan's magnum opus arrived in the form of "The IT Crowd," a 2006 Channel 4 sitcom that he both wrote and directed. Notably, Linehan chose to break away from the prevailing British trend of mockumentary-style comedies, opting instead for a traditional format. The show's unique charm lay in its recording before a live studio audience, a departure from the conventions of its time. His creative endeavor was duly recognized when he received an International Emmy in November 2008, a testament to the show's global appeal and comedic brilliance.

Linehan's creative output continued to flourish with "The Walshes" in 2013, a sitcom he wrote and directed. He also co-wrote the first series of the BBC sitcom "Motherland" and directed its pilot episode, showcasing his versatility as a writer and director in the comedy genre.

A highlight in Linehan's illustrious career came in 2014 when he clinched his fifth BAFTA, this time in the category of Best Writer, Comedy, for his outstanding contributions to "The IT Crowd." Notably, he was also nominated for his work on "Count Arthur Strong," further underscoring his enduring impact on the world of British comedy.

Through this rich tapestry of projects, Graham Linehan's creative genius has left an indelible mark on the world of comedy, demonstrating his ability to craft humor that resonates with audiences both in the UK and beyond.

Expanding Horizons

Father Ted and Other Iconic Shows

In the realm of creative ambitions, 2018 marked an exciting chapter for Graham Linehan and Arthur Mathews as they unveiled their ambitious project: a **"Father Ted"** musical. This announcement carried a profound sense of nostalgia and closure, as it aimed to realize the conclusion of the beloved series as originally envisioned before the untimely passing of its lead actor, Dermot Morgan.

The musical was poised to offer fans of "Father Ted" a chance to revisit the iconic world of Craggy Island and its unforgettable characters, all while delivering the humor and wit that had endeared the show to audiences worldwide. It was a heartfelt endeavor that sought to pay homage to the show's legacy while offering a new and exciting dimension to the "Father Ted" story.

However, the trajectory of this musical project took an unexpected turn when controversy engulfed Linehan due to his outspoken views on transgender rights. The divisive nature of his advocacy caused ripples in various spheres, ultimately leading to the cancellation of the "Father Ted" musical by the producers. This decision was a reflection of the complexities surrounding Linehan's public persona and the challenging balance between creative endeavors and contentious ideologies.

In this narrative, the "Father Ted" musical journey, although promising, faced an unfortunate and untimely end, serving as a poignant reminder of the intricate interplay between personal beliefs and creative pursuits in the world of entertainment.

The creative minds behind some of the most iconic British comedies, Graham Linehan and Arthur Mathews, have made memorable cameo appearances in the very programs they've penned, adding an extra layer of humor and familiarity for fans.

In the classic sitcom "I'm Alan Partridge," Linehan and Mathews made a humorous appearance as two Irish TV producers. Their characters were considering the hapless Alan Partridge, portrayed by Steve Coogan, for a potential contract, resulting in a delightful collision of comedic talents.

Linehan's penchant for on-screen appearances extended beyond "I'm Alan Partridge." He made notable cameos in several productions, adding his unique flair to the shows. In "The Day Today," a satirical news program,

Linehan made his mark, infusing his humor into the fabric of the show. Additionally, he graced two episodes of "Garth Marenghi's Darkplace" with his presence, contributing to the offbeat humor of this cult classic.

Fans of "Black Books" might remember Linehan's brief appearances in the series. In series one, episode two, he hilariously played the "I love books" Guy, and in series one, episode five, he made a cameo as a Fast Food Customer, leaving his imprint on the comedic landscape of the show.

Linehan's connection to "Father Ted" extended beyond his writing duties. He made memorable appearances in several episodes of the series, including "Good Luck Father Ted," "Entertaining Father Stone," "Flight Into Terror," "Cigarettes, Alcohol and Rollerblading," and "Chirpy Burpy Cheap Sheep," adding his comedic touch to the beloved show.

Notably, Linehan also featured in four episodes of "The IT Crowd," a series he both wrote and directed. His cameo roles ranged from playing Messy Joe's Restaurant Musician in series one, episode three, to a blind sorcerer in series two, episode six. He even appeared as Beth Gaga Shaggy in series four, episode three, showcasing his versatility as a performer.

Linehan's presence in the world of British comedy extended to panel shows, including "Never Mind the Buzzcocks," where he participated in the Identity Parade round, offering his comedic insights. He also made his mark in the pilot and series of "Little Britain," assuming various roles that added depth to the show's humor.

In sum, Graham Linehan's comedic talents and versatility were not confined to the writer's chair; he made delightful cameo appearances that enriched the humor and charm of the shows he helped create.

On Radio

Graham Linehan's foray into the world of radio brought with it a memorable and thought-provoking moment on the BBC Radio 4's "Today" program.

On June 6, 2011, Linehan graced the airwaves to discuss his adaptation of the classic Ealing comedy film, "The Ladykillers," for the West End stage. However, what unfolded during this radio appearance was a spirited exchange, not about the adaptation itself, but rather, a disagreement between Linehan and the "Today" program's presenter, Justin Webb. Linehan perceived

Webb's approach as an attempt to orchestrate an artificial argument, particularly with the critic Michael Billington.

This clash of perspectives left Linehan questioning the format and integrity of such contrived confrontations within the media. He expanded on his critique in an article published in The Guardian, expressing his frustration with what he saw as a narrow, binary approach to presenting arguments, whether in politics or in broader life discussions. Linehan's assertion was that this format oversimplified complex issues and created an artificial sense of polarization, which, in his view, was not conducive to meaningful discourse.

His call for change was clear: Linehan advocated for a more nuanced, authentic, and honest approach to public conversations, one that transcended the limitations of a binary framework. His criticism underscored his commitment to thoughtful and meaningful discourse, even in the realm of radio broadcasting.

Later Project:Continuing Work In Television

Graham Linehan's multifaceted career and creative endeavors continued to evolve and diversify, leaving a distinctive mark in various fields.

One particularly heartwarming episode in his creative journey occurred in the animated series "Adventure Time." In the 2012 episode titled "Goliad," Linehan's own children lent their voices to characters, with their father, Linehan, taking on the directorial role. Remarkably, during this creative process, Linehan directed his children's performances while simultaneously receiving instructions from the producers over the phone. This familial collaboration added a personal and endearing touch to the episode and showcased Linehan's ability to seamlessly merge his personal and professional life.

Linehan's creative ambitions extended further as he planned to write a sequel episode for "Adventure Time." He dedicated time and effort to crafting different versions of the story and enthusiastically shared them with the production team. Regrettably, the sequel episode never came to fruition, as "Adventure Time" concluded its run in 2018.

In 2023, Linehan explored yet another facet of his comedic talents by taking to the stage for a stand-up comedy set at the Backyard Comedy Club in London. This move allowed him to connect with live audiences, delivering his unique brand of humor in person and showcasing his versatility as a comedian.

Moreover, the anticipation surrounding Linehan's upcoming memoir, titled "Tough Crowd: How I Made and Lost a Career in Comedy," reached a fever pitch ahead of its publication in September 2023. Impressively, the memoir secured the second-highest number of pre-orders on Amazon, a testament to Linehan's ability to captivate audiences not only through his performances but also through his written reflections on his life and career.

In summary, Graham Linehan's creative journey continued to unfold, with each endeavor offering new insights into his diverse talents and unwavering dedication to the world of entertainment. His ability to connect with audiences, whether through animated collaborations, stand-up comedy, or the written word, remains a testament to his enduring impact on the world of comedy and entertainment.

ACTIVISM AND CONTROVERSIES

Graham Linehan's public persona has become synonymous with his involvement in anti-transgender activism, a topic that has stirred significant debate and controversy.

The genesis of Linehan's involvement in this activism can be traced back to a 2008 episode of "The IT Crowd" titled "The Speech," which he wrote. When the episode was rebroadcast in 2013, it sparked widespread criticism for its perceived transphobic and sexist content. Critics argued that it relied on gender stereotypes and trivialized violence against transgender women. In the episode, a man discovers that his girlfriend is transgender, leading to a confrontation. The backlash against the episode's content and themes prompted Channel 4 to remove it from circulation in 2020.

Linehan, however, defended the episode, maintaining that he did not comprehend the intensity of the response and asserting that the humor was intended to be "harmless." He contended that a transphobic character within the episode did not render the entire production transphobic.

His skepticism extended to the concept of gender self-identification, with Linehan expressing objections to what he perceived as "privileged white people" demanding unquestioning acceptance of self-identified gender. He emphasized that individuals experiencing gender dysphoria should receive support and assistance but voiced concerns about early interventions for children undergoing transgender processes.

Linehan's critique of what he referred to as "trans ideology" became prominent on the social network Twitter. He contended that this ideology misrepresented transgender individuals and lesbians, sparking further debate and polarization within the online discourse surrounding transgender rights.

In essence, Graham Linehan's involvement in anti-transgender activism has placed him at the center of a contentious and emotionally charged debate. His positions on issues related to gender identity and transgender rights have ignited passionate discussions and have been met with both support and criticism from various quarters.

Before First Twitter Ban

Prior to his first Twitter ban, Graham Linehan found himself embroiled in a series of controversies and legal disputes that revolved around his vocal stance on transgender issues.

In 2018, Linehan publicly praised anti-transgender protesters who had participated in that year's London Pride event. These protesters had carried banners and distributed flyers with messages such as "transactivism erases lesbians," a viewpoint that Linehan endorsed, referring to them as "heroes." This public endorsement of a controversial stance drew attention and intensified the ongoing discourse surrounding transgender rights.

Later in the same year, Stephanie Hayden, a transgender woman, initiated a legal action against Linehan, accusing him of harassment. Hayden alleged that Linehan had used his Twitter platform to share personal photos from her life before transitioning, insinuated that she was involved in criminal activities, and repeatedly misgendered and deadnamed her. In response, Linehan claimed that Hayden had made public several private addresses associated with his family, ostensibly in an attempt to silence him. Law enforcement issued Linehan a verbal warning, cautioning him against further contact with Hayden.

In a December 2018 interview with Derrick Jensen, Linehan made controversial remarks about the transgender movement and likened it to providing "cover" for what he described as "fetishists, con men, and simply abusive misogynists." These statements added fuel to the already heated debate surrounding transgender rights and representation.

In a subsequent interview with the BBC program Newsnight in February 2020, Linehan escalated the controversy by comparing the Tavistock Centre's practice of administering puberty blockers to children to Nazi eugenics and experiments on children. This analogy drew sharp criticism, with Eric Pickles, the United Kingdom Special Envoy for Post-Holocaust Issues, accusing Linehan of trivializing the Holocaust, an assertion that further intensified the debate surrounding his views.

In essence, prior to his initial Twitter ban, Graham Linehan's outspoken stance on transgender issues and his involvement in contentious legal disputes placed him at the center of a highly polarized and emotionally charged conversation surrounding transgender rights, activism, and representation.

In January 2019, Graham Linehan voiced his concerns over the news that Mermaids, a charitable advocacy organization supporting transgender children and teenagers, was set to receive a £500,000 lottery grant aimed at establishing clinics across the United Kingdom. Linehan took to the blogging platform Mumsnet to encourage its users to lobby the National Lottery Community Fund with the aim of reversing this decision. Despite his efforts, the grant was ultimately reviewed and approved.

In response to Linehan's actions, YouTuber Hbomberguy organized a remarkable 57-hour fundraising livestream that managed to raise an additional £270,000 in support of Mermaids. This unexpected surge of donations demonstrated the depth of support for organizations like Mermaids within certain online communities.

During the same year, British journalist Dawn Foster accused Linehan and others of targeting an employee of the National Society for the Prevention of Cruelty to Children (NSPCC) who had been responsible for hiring Munroe Bergdorf, a transgender woman and activist. Foster characterized the online attacks as "transphobic" and "flatly homophobic," while journalist Chris Godfrey labeled the treatment of the employee as "insidious homophobia." These accusations highlighted the divisive and at times hostile nature of the debate surrounding transgender issues.

In June 2020, Linehan found himself once again in the midst of a controversy when he criticized comments made by author J.K. Rowling, who was widely perceived as transphobic. He shared a blog post featuring screenshots of abusive messages directed at Rowling and criticized those who authored them for what he saw as a lack of attention to the abuse received by women who spoke out against certain gender ideology. His comments prompted a response from musician Hozier, who accused Linehan of engaging in an "obsessive little culture war."

These incidents underscored the ongoing tension and polarization surrounding transgender rights, activism, and representation, with Linehan consistently taking a vocal and contentious stance within this charged discourse.

Controversies Surrounding Linehan's View

Graham Linehan's turbulent relationship with social media platforms, particularly Twitter, continued to be a focal point of controversy.

On June 27, 2020, Linehan's Twitter account faced a permanent suspension by the platform. Twitter cited "repeated violations of our rules against hateful conduct and platform manipulation" as the reason for the suspension. This move came after Linehan had been involved in numerous contentious online debates, particularly related to transgender issues.

In December of the same year, Linehan resurfaced on Twitter under an account posing as a transgender man, effectively evading his suspension. He used this account to criticize Colm O'Gorman, accusing him of being "a traitor to women, gay people, and yourself" for signing an open letter published by the Transgender Equality Network of Ireland. Twitter subsequently banned this account as well, but Linehan stated that he had created another one.

A significant turn of events occurred in December 2022 when Twitter underwent changes following its takeover by Elon Musk. Musk relaxed some of Twitter's content policies and announced an amnesty to restore suspended accounts, leading to the restoration of Linehan's Twitter account.

In February 2021, Linehan stirred further controversy when he created a fake account on the lesbian dating app Her and publicly shared screenshots of non-binary individuals and transgender women who were using the platform. The developers of Her promptly clarified that transgender women are welcome on the app.

March 2021 saw Linehan giving oral evidence to the Communications and Digital Committee of the House of Lords, focusing on the topic of freedom of expression online. During his testimony, he highlighted his use of Twitter to draw attention to what he described as "an all-out assault on women, on their words, their dignity, and their safety."

Throughout these events, Graham Linehan's actions and statements on social media platforms remained a source of intense debate and scrutiny, reflecting the broader conversations and challenges surrounding freedom of expression, online discourse, and transgender rights.

Graham Linehan's outspoken views and activism continued to influence his career choices and public statements.

In an interview with the Irish Independent, Linehan made it clear that he had ruled out the possibility of working with Channel 4 again. This decision was rooted in the network's refusal to return the controversial "The IT Crowd" episode to broadcast circulation. Additionally, he expressed a similar stance toward the BBC, citing their depiction of a transgender lesbian couple in a CBeebies video as a "heterosexual couple." These stances reflected Linehan's strong convictions on transgender issues and his willingness to take a stand even at the cost of professional collaborations.

Leading up to the 2022 Australian federal election in May, Linehan leveraged his online platforms to garner international support for the Liberal Party candidate Katherine Deves. Deves had generated controversy due to her anti-transgender comments, and Linehan's public endorsement added fuel to the ongoing debates surrounding transgender rights and political discourse.

In September 2022, Linehan made a surprising statement, indicating that his involvement in anti-transgender activism had led him to question the safety of COVID-19 vaccinations and the scientific consensus on climate change. He expressed feelings of betrayal, stating that he had been "lied to so conclusively by all the people [he] used to trust." These remarks demonstrated the profound impact that his advocacy and engagement in contentious debates had on his broader worldview.

Graham Linehan's activism and strong convictions continued to shape his career choices and public statements, leading him to take decisive positions on a range of issues, from transgender rights and political endorsements to his views on COVID-19 vaccinations and climate change. These positions placed him at the center of complex and polarizing debates, reflecting the enduring influence of his advocacy work.

In interviews conducted in 2022 and 2023, Graham Linehan candidly expressed how the debate surrounding transgender issues had profoundly impacted his life. He conveyed that this ongoing debate had consumed much of his time and attention, resulting in significant personal and professional consequences.

Linehan revealed that his involvement in the debate had cost him job opportunities and financial stability, and had even led to the dissolution of his marriage. One notable setback was the cancellation of the Father Ted musical, a project on which Linehan had been financially dependent. The production company had determined that his involvement would render the musical impossible to stage.

Prior to the cancellation of the musical, Linehan had taken a strong stance on the issue of transgender rights within the project. He had called on all individuals working on the musical to sign a declaration that aligned with some of his views on transgender people. He had also disclosed clashes with colleagues over their differing views on trans rights. Linehan had conveyed his concerns to his collaborators in a letter, expressing doubt that they had his full support as collaborators, business partners, or friends. He asserted that he and J.K. Rowling had been vindicated in their belief that what they saw as a "poisonous ideology" was causing harm to individuals' lives.

Linehan attributed his situation to what he referred to as "cancel culture." He contended that comedians and other public figures were constantly navigating a climate where certain issues had become hot-button topics, and deviating from an accepted narrative could result in reputational damage or career setbacks. He expressed a belief that this climate placed undue pressure on individuals to conform to a specific viewpoint.

In 2023, Linehan sought to clarify his stance, emphasizing that he did not dislike transgender people but held opposing views on using their preferred pronouns, which he considered "immoral." He clarified that he did not take issue with individuals identifying as a different gender but was specifically concerned with areas where conflicts arose in this context.

In sum, Graham Linehan's involvement in the transgender rights debate had profound and far-reaching effects on his personal and professional life. His experiences served as a reflection of the complex and contentious nature of the discourse surrounding transgender issues and the impact it can have on individuals' careers, relationships, and worldviews.

After Being Reinstated on Twitter

Following his previous suspension Graham Linehan's return to Twitter in December 2022 brought with it a new set of controversies and conflicts.

One incident that drew criticism involved Linehan mocking contestants and writers on the quiz show "Only Connect" for their sexualities and gender identities. Victoria Coren Mitchell, who hosts the show, called him out on Twitter, urging him to "leave them alone." Linehan's comments, targeting individuals based on their personal attributes, sparked backlash and added to the ongoing discussions about the boundaries of free expression on social media.

Linehan also engaged in a heated exchange with Ian "H" Watkins of the band Steps. Linehan tweeted a question insinuating a connection between Watkins and a convicted criminal based on Watkins' use of a tool to block individuals he considered transphobic. This exchange exemplified the contentious nature of Linehan's online interactions, particularly when it came to transgender-related issues.

In April 2023, Linehan found himself banned from Twitter once again. This occurred after his participation in an anti-trans event called "Let Women Speak" in Belfast, Northern Ireland. In response to a Twitter user referencing counter-protestors at the event, Linehan tweeted the words ``Durr i'm gonna kill em,'' leading to his account being suspended. His account was later reinstated a few days later.

Another controversy emerged in July 2023 when Linehan took to Twitter to accuse actor David Tennant of being an "abusive groomer." This accusation stemmed from photos of Tennant wearing a T-shirt with the message "Leave Trans Kids Alone You Absolute

Freaks." Tennant's public support for transgender rights and his stance on protecting transgender children had prompted Linehan's provocative remark.

These incidents highlighted the ongoing tensions surrounding Linehan's online presence, reflecting the broader debate over the boundaries of free speech, hate speech, and the responsibilities of social media platforms in moderating content.

The vivid drama of August 2023 unfolded during the Edinburgh Festival Fringe, a time when creativity and laughter usually took center stage. However, for Graham Linehan, a controversial figure embroiled in the stormy sea of public opinion, this festival would be a departure from the norm.

As the festival buzzed with anticipation, Linehan and a cadre of fellow comedians found themselves in an unexpected predicament. Their original bookings for comedy gigs had been abruptly canceled by venues, all due to the contentious nature of Linehan's views on various issues, particularly transgender rights. Undeterred by this setback, they decided to take their comedy act to a different kind of stage—one far more symbolic.

Their unconventional choice was the exterior of the Scottish Parliament, a hallowed ground where political discourse usually reigned supreme. Here, under the open sky and against the backdrop of one of Scotland's most iconic institutions, Linehan and his comrades would make their comedic stand. It was a theatrical twist in the ongoing saga of Linehan's public persona.

As they performed their stand-up comedy show, an eclectic audience gathered. Among them were Linehan's steadfast supporters, individuals who stood by his side despite the controversy that swirled around him. Some in the crowd weren't just there for the humor; they were there to make a statement. They believed that the Edinburgh Fringe had become overly sensitive, a place where the boundaries of comedy and free expression were being tested and, in their view, strained to the point of rupture.

The festival, known for celebrating artistic freedom, now found itself facing criticism from those who believed it had become too cautious, too quick to bow to the pressures of political correctness. Linehan's outdoor performance outside the Scottish Parliament symbolized a clash of ideologies and a quest to reclaim a sense of humor in an environment where controversy often overshadowed comedy.

In a bold move, Linehan also issued a legal threat. He threatened to sue the first venue that had canceled his gig, making it clear that he was willing to challenge the consequences of his outspoken views in court.

Amidst this tumultuous backdrop, Linehan penned an article for The Telegraph, offering a glimpse into his inner turmoil. He spoke of his exhaustion with the constant battles and protests, revealing a longing for the simpler days of comedy—a sentiment that resonated with those who had followed his journey.

In sum, the Edinburgh Festival Fringe of August 2023 became an unexpected stage for Graham Linehan's ongoing narrative. It was a tale of defiance, support, criticism, legal threats, and a yearning for the laughter that had once defined his career. Against the historic backdrop of the Scottish Parliament, the clash of sensibilities and the desire for a return to comedy took center stage in a story that was far from reaching its final act.

INFLUENCES AND IMPACTS

Graham Linehan, the renowned Irish comedy writer and creator of beloved TV series like "Father Ted," "Black Books," and "The IT Crowd," has left an indelible mark on the world of comedy and entertainment. His comedic style, characterized by its dark, subversive, and often absurd humor, has not only earned critical acclaim but has also influenced a generation of comedians and writers.

Linehan's unique brand of humor often delves into taboo subjects and pushes the boundaries of comedy. This fearlessness in exploring unconventional and edgy comedic terrain has served as an inspiration for many comedians seeking to challenge the status quo.

His shows are celebrated for their well-developed and eccentric characters. From Bernard Black in "Black Books" to Ted Crilly in "Father Ted" and Roy Trenneman in "The IT Crowd," Linehan's ability to create complex, flawed, yet relatable characters has set a high standard for character-driven comedy.

Linehan's collaborative approach to creativity has also left a significant impact. His partnerships with co-writers and talented actors have resulted in comedy gold. This emphasis on teamwork and the synergy between writers and performers has influenced how comedy is conceived and produced in the industry.

Throughout his career, Linehan has fearlessly addressed sensitive and controversial topics in his shows, including religion, identity, and societal norms. By using humor as a tool to challenge conventions, he has encouraged other comedians to do the same, sparking important conversations through comedy.

Linehan's work has transcended borders and found international audiences. His shows have been exported and adapted in various countries, highlighting the universal appeal of his humor. This global reach has paved the way for comedians from different cultures to explore similar comedic sensibilities.

Moreover, Linehan's legacy endures as his work continues to inspire a new generation of comedians and writers. His shows remain relevant and attract viewers, introducing his unique comedic style to younger audiences. Many contemporary comedians acknowledge Linehan as a significant influence on their own work, demonstrating his enduring impact on the comedy landscape.

In conclusion, Graham Linehan's legacy in the world of comedy is defined by his fearless humor, unforgettable characters, and the enduring popularity of his shows. His influence can be seen in the edgier, character-driven comedy that characterizes contemporary television. Linehan's contribution to the industry and his ability to provoke thought while eliciting laughter have cemented his status as a comedy icon.

Printed in Great Britain
by Amazon

30959586R00030